[SECOND EDITION. 35TH THOUSAND.]

Everybody's Book

OF

Correct Conduct,

BEING

The Etiquette of Every-day Life.

BY M. C.

London:

SAXON & CO.

23,
BOUVERIE ST.,
FLEET ST., E.C.

PRYOR PUBLICATIONS
WHITSTABLE AND WALSALL

MEMBER OF
INDEPENDENT PUBLISHERS GUILD

© 1995 Pryor Publications
75 Dargate Road, Yorkletts, Whitstable,
Kent CT5 3AE, England.
Tel. & Fax: (01227) 274655
Specialists in Facsimile Reproductions.

Reprinted 1996

ISBN 0 946014 37 X

A CIP Record for this book is avaialble from the British Library.

First Published 1893

Printed and bound by
Biddles Ltd.

Woodbridge Park Estate,
Woodbridge Road,
Guildford GU1 1DA

Preface.

THIS little volume is intended as a guide in every-day conduct in all matters, and at the same time as a mentor in the important affairs of life. It is certain that he who lives correctly every day will find himself following the higher laws of morality and rectitude. As a preceptor for young and old alike, it will be found invaluable, giving as it does the rules to be observed by children in their conduct towards their parents, and the duties of parents towards their children. It goes into the etiquette of entertaining and visiting thoroughly, and will be found most useful either to the inexperienced hostess or to the visitor unaccustomed to society. In the relations between husband and wife it gives rules which will induce and preserve harmony; to the business man it teaches a code which will win for him respect as well as success; and to the sportsman it imparts the necessary guidance in conduct which will enable him to obtain both pleasure and popularity. No part of daily life has been omitted, and it is confidently hoped that the book will be found to fill a vacant place in education, and assist both teachers of others and teachers of themselves in their task.

THE AUTHOR.

January, 1893.

Contents.

PART I.

The Duties of Life.

CHAPTER I.

IN THE HOME CIRCLE.

It is the correct thing

To be as courteous, considerate, affable, and entertaining at home as in society.

For a man to consider that money spent to give pleasure to his wife and family is money well spent.

For every member of the family to remember that the maxim, "Bear and forbear," is as important in dealing with one's own relations as with strangers.

For the women of the household to make it pleasant and attractive, and for the men to show their appreciation of these efforts.

For every room in the house to be as attractive and agreeable, in their different styles, as the drawing room in which visitors are received.

To be ever ready and glad to give a place at the table to a friend.

To remember that open-handed hospitality is usually only rewarded by the pleasure it gives, and to expect no other.

To remember that a happy and harmonious home rears great and noble men and women; and that the friend who visits is often influenced by its atmosphere to good.

To let no unpleasant subject be broached at table, or in the evenings, if possible. Painful discussions, such as must sometimes arise in a family, can be kept to their own time and place, and not allowed to mar the happiness of those not immediately concerned.

To remember that punctuality is a virtue which cannot be dispensed with in a comfortable household, and is as important a duty as any with a finer sounding name;

without it no house can be kept in order and comfort.

For the younger members of the family to give place to the elder, the stronger to the weaker, as in society; the same rules of courtesy should be observed.

For the father, husband, brothers to show the same respect and courtesy to the ladies of the household in everything as they would to any other ladies of their acquaintance; especially so in the presence of children or servants.

To remember that the lady who rules the household must have absolute authority in it and rule as absolute queen. No comfort or order can be obtained without this. If her orders are to be questioned, the correct thing is to do so in private, and never in the presence of the young members of the household, or of the servants.

For the lady who holds this position to remember that the every-day happiness of those in the home circle is in her hands;

that she has the greatest power of anyone to make the home a place of peace and happiness, or a place to avoid.

For a man, when he spends evenings at his club, or away from home, to remember that those left at home may have been very dull, and to try and compensate for his absence by bringing good humour and pleasant talk with him when he returns.

For every member of the circle to remember that a simple family meal may be made as delightful a gathering as a set dinner-party, if all come to it with the intention of making it so.

It is not the correct thing

To suppose that only the rich can have happy or agreeable homes. It is often in very simple households that the finest manners are found, and consequently the greatest happiness is found in them also.

To lay aside good manners with one's

walking dress, as if only intended for use in the outer world.

To imagine that little quarrels, or unpleasant discussions over small matters, are of no consequence. Too often they alienate those who loved each other as time goes on, and frequently drive those who are free to leave it from a home in which they would otherwise be happy.

To spend money in small pleasures beyond what the income can afford; but neither is it the correct thing for the head of a household, who can permit himself expensive wines and cigars, to grudge his wife and daughters sweets and flowers and pretty clothes.

To be careless in dress at home any more than when abroad. The dress should be appropriate to the occasion, and all the better if it is; but dressing-gown and slippers, working dress or morning wrapper, can all be as fresh and becoming as evening dress. This is one of the most important rules in the home circle, both for men and women.

B

To be indifferent and selfish in small matters. Coldness and carelessness destroy the charm of home life.

To sacrifice comfort for the sake of appearances.

To be a gourmand at the family dinner-table any more than at a social one.

To allow children to be out of their place and an annoyance to the grown-up members of the family any more than to visitors. It makes themselves unhappy in the end as well as those who weary of them.

CHAPTER II.

AS A HUSBAND.

It is the correct thing

To marry for love; and if you have not
done so, to treat your wife with the same
courtesy and gentleness as though you had,
both before others and when alone.

To remember that, if you consider your wife
the weaker vessel, for that very reason you
should treat her with consideration.

To study to please her in all such matters
as do not involve a question of right and
wrong. In time she will perceive this, and
you will be amply repaid.

If your age is in excess of her own, it is
the correct thing for you to show her extra

consideration and care, as you have so much more knowledge of the world and its requirements than she can have.

If you are of the same age, to treat her as a friend and equal in all matters. This will win her affection in later years, when you will stand more in need of it than of anything else.

To be really attentive to her; for, if you are neglectful, it is only natural that she should turn elsewhere for attention. A husband's neglect leads to dire evils.

To be watchful of her comfort; small attentions win gratitude, and of gratitude love is sometimes born; by it it is certainly and surely retained.

To guard her; not as a slave, by tyranny or harshness, but like a jewel, with care and forethought.

To avoid making her suffer perhaps unnecessary jealousy by markedly admiring other women, or by relating anecdotes of former flirtations. This may give you a feeling of triumph at the moment, but in reality creates a gulf between yourself and your wife which will widen and bring misery.

It is most emphatically the correct thing to escort her to all public places, to accompany her into society, and to be with her on all possible occasions. A husband who is careless of this duty has only himself to blame if he loses his wife's affections, or if scandal attack her.

To give her as much amusement as you can afford ; that she is your wife is no reason for her to be dull or permitted to suffer from *ennui.*

To refrain from being jealous of old admirers, or worrying her with regard to them. She left them all for you, and if you bear this in mind you will see that to make her never regret it is your only right course.

To establish, in every-day life, a system of "give and take." If she yields her will in one small matter, yield yours in another; thus you will create a friendship far more valuable than even love itself.

To draw her confidence towards you, not to repel it by inquisitiveness or unreasonable jealousy.

It is not the correct thing

To treat your wife with a discourtesy you would not dare to show to a paid housekeeper; a fault too common among men who do not understand that happiness is to be obtained at home. There is no greater sign of ill-breeding in a man than rudeness towards the woman whom he has made a part of himself.

To leave your wife alone in the evenings, while you go to your club or to bachelor parties. If you do this, you must expect her either to seek amusement elsewhere, or she to be sulky and perhaps in tears when you return.

To storm and scold if dinner is five minutes late. Few men can say that they never keep the dinner waiting half an hour; and why should the housekeeper possess to perfection that virtue of punctuality which the business

man and bread-winner cannot always attain?
Some men think it right to treat their wives as
inferiors, and yet to expect superiority in them
in matters of this kind, just as some people
do with their servants.

To bring home unexpected guests, unless
your home and table are always conducted on
a scale to admit of it. Nothing mortifies a
hostess so much as to be unable to properly
entertain a visitor. It places her at a disadvantage which you, accustomed to club and
restaurant life, cannot possibly realise. A
sixpenny telegram will often save your wife
mortification, yourself discomfort, and your
guest disgust.

To be inconsistent, and, while spending
frequent evenings out yourself, think her
unreasonable if she wants your escort to a
ball, or wishes for theatre tickets.

To interfere in household management. If
you do this you should take it altogether. A
house can have but one ruler; and if you are
a business man you will readily apprehend

how impossible it would be to allow your wife to interfere at rare intervals in the office, putting all your *employés* out of humour by extraordinary orders, and then leaving you to get matters right again.

To use language which you would not care for her to adopt. Remember that the purest snow cannot help being tarred if touched with pitch.

To tell stories to her, or in her presence, which you would not care for her to repeat, for the same reason. If you do so, and she changes, alters, or deteriorates, you have only yourself to thank and cannot blame her.

CHAPTER III.

AS A WIFE.

It is the correct thing

To remember that, for whatever reason, your husband has paid you the compliment of selecting you out of the world of women, and that it lies with yourself to make him feel that in doing so he did right.

To realise that if your husband is to stay at home, his home must be attractive enough to keep him from the club and from his friends' houses.

To remember, if your income is small, that a prettily set table will make a simple meal agreeable, especially with a smiling face as its greatest ornament; and, if you are rich, that the best dinner in the world can be made distasteful by an exhibition of temper or ill-breeding.

To know that your rule is the rule of love. You may be, and should be, absolute despot, so long as your husband thinks you the most charming woman in the world. When you begin to rule in any other way, you may lose your sovereignty altogether, for you have stepped out of your place ; and then you must expect your husband to show a new side of his character to you, and must meet it as you best can.

To treat your husband always as your friend, and in doing this you will be careful never to forfeit his respect, or weary him by stories of little annoyances. Remember that a friend is of more value than a lover, and that, though you may tyrannise over a lover, you can only keep him at your feet as long as his passion lasts; while a real friend you keep for life, and the best one you can have is your own husband.

To remember that you do not pry into your *friends'* private affairs, or read their letters unless they ask you to, or cross-examine them as to how they spend their time when away from you; neither do you look into their pockets, or take their money without asking, or worry them unnecessarily about trifles.

To be as particular in your dress and in the arrangement of your hair for him at all hours when a husband, as you were at appointed hours when he was still a lover. This may make more difference in the ultimate happiness of your life than you can imagine.

To defend your husband under all circumstances and to all accusers. If he has done wrong, let him know you are aware of it when alone with him, but never admit it to others.

To resent any kind of disparagement of him, even from your own relations.

To be ready to please your husband in all matters, from the choice of your visitors to the choice of your gowns. For you two to agree makes life a pleasure, and the surren-

dering of your own caprices occasionally is a
very trifling price to pay for the sake of
harmony; while if you disagree, then your
union is a failure.

To be perfectly courteous to your husband
before guests, servants, or children, even if
there should be any matter of disagreement
between you. This courtesy you owe to him
and to yourself. Only a woman who has lost
her own self-respect will stoop to say unkind
things to her husband before outsiders. It is
ill-bred, because it is very painful to the
others, who are, of course, unable to enter into
the matter.

To give your husband the final authority
always, as the head of the house, and to
act always as though you and he are really
one.

If you follow these rules, society and Mrs.
Grundy can find no fault with you. Do not
break any of them without a certain convic-
tion that you are right in doing so. Many
young wives sacrifice a life's happiness

through mere thoughtlessness and ignorance of her duty.

It is not correct

To put any kind of slight upon your husband under any circumstances. To do this takes away from your dignity, not from his.

To disparage him in any way to others.

To allow him to see you worried, or crying over trifles. It will weary him of you sooner than anything else. It is the correct thing for you to make the sunshine of life for him, as he has all the responsibility, and must of necessity have many trials heavier than you can know of.

To expect your husband to be always at your side, or at home; he will value both you and the home more if he is free to come and go as he likes. Dismiss him with a smile, and receive him with one, and you will find he will return as quickly as he can for the sake of the sunshine you give him.

To laugh at your husband's little whims and refuse to indulge them, for you must remember that, though you are in authority at home, nevertheless he is the head of the house.

To go out into society without your husband at all; even to your own mother's house it is scarcely correct, if she has a formal party to which he has been invited. However much it may annoy you to stay at home, if he cannot go, remember that it is *not correct* to go without him.

To disregard him in society and flirt openly with other admirers. This is only done in fast sets, and although some husbands rather like to see their wives doing it, that does not alter the fact that it is not correct, and lowers you in the estimation of others.

CHAPTER IV.

BETWEEN PARENTS AND CHILDREN.

It is the correct thing

For parents and children to be good friends, and if there should unfortunately be any disagreement between them to conceal it in the presence of others.

For a young man to show respect to his father. Not to do so does not lessen the father's dignity, but shows that the son does not know what is good form.

For a young girl to give her mother the deference due to her. It is undeniable that the young sometimes possess qualities their elders have not, talents being inborn. A girl may be a better housekeeper than her mother, a better accountant, or more accomplished; but if she exhibits her talents in such a way as to imply a contempt for her mother, it will only make onlookers dislike her, in spite of her ability.

To remember that to be a good son or a good daughter is a lovable trait, and inclines other persons to like you. The old adage that "a good son makes a good husband" is so true that no one can afford to forget it.

To remember, if you are a parent, that to your children you stand first in the place of God, and afterwards in that of their nearest and dearest of friends. If they cannot come to you in childhood with perfect confidence in your judgment, justice, and mercy, to whom are they to go? Betray a child's trust and you inflict on it a life-long wrong.

To remember, as they grow older, that what they need is friendship and sympathy. When young people find these in their parents it prevents their going into the world for friendship while still too young to discriminate between good and bad acquaintances.

To know that a contempt for the tie of blood shows a heartlessness certain to be rewarded by solitude late in life. That " blood is thicker than water " is another true axiom never to be forgotten.

For a parent to show pride in his children ; not to do so is to be unnatural. But it is not the correct thing for you to imagine that other people are as interested in them as you are. How should it be so ? It is the blood-tie which makes them so dear.

For children to speak even more lovingly and respectfully of their parents in their absence than in their presence. This will endear you to others, for it shows a true heart.

For parents to remember that the young have to buy their own experience. This is a law of nature which cannot be altered.

For children to accept their parents' judgment as worthy of respect, if only because they have travelled so much further on in life

C

and necessarily know more of its pitfalls and snares.

When in society, for a young man to give his mother as much attention, and show her as much courtesy, as if she were his sweetheart. Among highly-bred persons you will always find this the custom.

At your father's dinner-table, to let him speak, and tell his own tales, without your interruption. If your generation is much more enlightened than his, it will not justify you in showing him any disrespect; and, perhaps, for all you know, the guests may really prefer his conversation.

CHAPTER V.

IN BUSINESS.

It is the correct thing

To make the utmost use of one's opportunities, and to get the best of a bargain if possible; but only so far as is consistent with being an honest man and a gentleman.

To remember that under all circumstances, and in every business transaction, it is necessary to act as a gentleman.

To be absolutely punctual. It is inconsistent to exact punctuality from subordinates unless you observe it yourself; and in important negotiations five minutes' delay will sometimes alter the whole face of affairs.

To hold one's word as sacred as one's bond.

For professional men to remember that confidences given to them in their professional capacities are absolutely secrets of honour. It is the correct thing to keep these perfectly sacred, even from one's own nearest and dearest and most trusted.

For business men to keep the discussion of matters of business entirely to that part of the day devoted to them, which is the best and largest portion. It is out of place to talk of business at a dinner-party; and to discuss it before your wife, if she does not enter into it, is as much a *gaucherie* as for her to regale you with gossip about the servants.

In business transactions, while it is right to keep one's own counsel, and sometimes to preserve a wise silence, yet it is necessary for a gentleman to avoid any misrepresentation. The line between misrepresentation and untruthfulness is very narrow.

To remember that adulation to power and arrogance to poverty mark a plebian in mind as well as in origin.

It is not the correct thing

For a man to think that he can be a gentleman in the drawing room and a boor and tyrant in his office. It is impossible to keep the two characters separate always.

To consider ignorance in another as a warrant for one's own imposition on him.

To forget that misrepresentation in a business man is first cousin to stealing.

To act as if might made right.

To forget that money paid in salaries to deserving men is not a kind of charity, but a positively good investment.

To forget that Fortune knocks once at every man's door, and sometimes only once.

To permit the growth of any irregular habits in business, either with regard to answering correspondence, keeping exactly punctual hours, or any other matters of detail.

To be a Shylock in demanding the uttermost farthing and the last drop of blood; remember always that business reverses may any day bring you into the position of the debtor, when you will remember the words, " Do as you would be done by."

To avoid all transactions that are considered as shady, for they will never be found to be of any use in the end.

PART II.

The Pleasures of Life.

CHAPTER I.

MAKING CALLS.

The correct thing

Is, first of all, to go at an opportune hour, when you know your hostess is disengaged and glad to see visitors. Most ladies who have a large circle of acquaintance give up one afternoon in the week or in the month to receiving their friends. If you are on the visiting list of a lady, you will receive a card on which the date of her day "at home" will be written, or perhaps printed. This is an excellent fashion, as it ensures your not wasting your visit (and if your hostess is an agreeable person, and you go from one end of London to the other to call on her, this is a consideration), and saves a great deal of her time. Nothing fritters so much time away as desultory calls. Therefore it is the correct thing for a lady to choose "a day," and keep to it, and for a visitor to be careful to respect her day and hour.

It is quite correct, if you wish to call on a lady who has perhaps given you an invitation to dinner, or whose acquaintance you wish to cultivate, to say to her (if you have not received a card), "What is your day?" If she then mentions a day, you are privileged to call on that day thenceforward.

It is the correct thing

To put all your "at home" cards on the mantel-shelf of your own room, or stick them into your looking-glass, and you will find it a most useful practice. It is not for show, but use. You want to be able to refer to them when you are going out visiting. If you go, calling at the right day and hour, you will be welcome as flowers in May; but if you rashly go at another time, you will feel, however amiable your hostess may be, that you are not wanted.

If you find a crowd of other callers, as you probably will, merely to exchange a few words with your hostess, and then to enter into conversation with anyone else you may happen to know who is present. If you do not see a familiar face at once, withdraw a little, and look around you. Do not attempt to monopolise your hostess, as her duties on these formal calling-days are as heavy as at an evening party.

On a recognised afternoon at home, when you call, to leave your hat and overcoat in the hall as you enter. While you are still a comparative stranger it is correct to keep your hat in your hand, but do not cumber yourself with anything else. You will readily understand that is correct, if you imagine your hostess receiving fifty gentlemen in the afternoon. If they all burdened themselves with hats, coats, and umbrellas, her drawing-room would look like a vestibule. When you have called on the lady once or twice, and feel that you are on her visiting list, leave your hat outside the drawing-room. Your gloves are a sufficient certificate to the other visitors that you, like themselves, are a visitor.

For a lady, when making such calls, to go in straight from the street in her wraps, and bonnet, and muff, if it be winter; in the summer, parasol or fan in hand. If, however, she is driving, and wears a carriage-wrap, that should be left in the carriage; if she is walking, and in wet weather wears a macintosh to cover her toilette, or in summer a dust-cloak, a wrap of this kind should be thrown off in the hall.

To wait for the servant to announce your name, and pause behind him or her until it is announced (whether heard or not, does not matter—if music or lively conversation are going on, it is not likely to be heard); then go forward and seek out your hostess. However intimate you may become at the house you are visiting, on the formal "at home" days this is the correct thing to do. You only show yourself at a disadvantage, and embarrass your hostess, if you open the drawing-room door and walk in unannounced. Remember this, even in visiting at a little suburban villa, where the drawing-room door is close to your hand as you enter; for if you go in unannounced, you give the impression that you are on the most intimate terms with the family. On a "formal day," only a brother or first cousin may do this.

To do anything you can to amuse the other visitors on a calling-day, if your hostess asks you. If you can sing, play, or recite, or have any other specialty, be sure you do not refuse her if she herself asks you to exercise your talent. That is a certain sign that her guests want amusing; and if you are complaisant and able to do what she wants, you will make a friend of her and always be a welcome guest, for sometimes it is most difficult for a hostess to keep a host of stray callers amused. There-

fore do not let any timidity or false pride
stand in your way; remember that a request
from your hostess is a command; this, of
course, provided she is previously aware of
your ability.

Even if calling on your own sister, on a
formal day, to preserve a society manner, and
never to introduce private or family topics of
conversation. To do so is quite as wanting in
taste and tact as, if you are a business man,
talking "shop." Society, remember, is a
region in which politeness is the first law. If
you outrage this, you will still live, of course;
but society will avoid you for its own sake.

Always to pay a visit of ceremony after an
invitation to dinner, or to a dance, whether
accepted or not. If the lady has a "day" be
sure and go then; if not, you may go on the
very first afternoon you can, even the next day.

It is not the correct thing

To make a visit of ceremony before four

o'clock in the afternoon; the best time is about five.

To take anyone with you, even on an "at home" afternoon, without previously asking your hostess's permission, or unless your intimacy with the family justifies your doing so. This is, however, a convenient method of making persons, hitherto stangers, acquainted; and if you happen to know someone clever, talented, or a "lion," you may make your hostess really grateful by taking him to one of her "afternoons." But, even so, it is not correct to do this without previously asking her permission.

To "perform" in any way, however talented you may be, except at your hostess's especial request, and not then unless both you and she are convinced of your ability. If, without knowing whether you can sing or play, she is foolish enough to ask you, do not comply unless your powers have been approved by others as well as yourself. If you perform badly you will find that you have received your last invitation and your last "at home" card.

To overstay the hour written on your hostess's card by one minute. Do not arrive too soon, or leave too late. This will not prevent your staying long enough to show that you have enjoyed your visit, always the correct thing to do when visiting.

CHAPTER II.

AS A HOST (OR HOSTESS).

It is the correct thing

To be hospitable and to entertain with discretion, but not to keep open house. No one values invitations that are extended to all.

In sending out invitations for a dinner-party, for the hostess to write notes of invitation herself—with her own hand; the same holds good for *an informal* dinner or luncheon, as it is the personal invitation which constitutes the compliment.

In issuing invitations for a large afternoon at home, an evening reception, a dance, a ball, or a garden-party, to send printed cards.

D

which are prettily prepared now by all good stationers. The date has to be filled in, and the name of the person to whom the card is sent written on the left-hand top corner, " Mrs. ——," "Mr. ——," or, in the case of a married couple, " Mr. and Mrs. ——," and this can be done by anyone, as the hostess's handwriting is not a necessity, which saves her a great deal of labour. If she has a properly kept visiting list a secretary can do all the writing. If there is any special feature about the entertainment a word indicating it should be written at the bottom of the card, on the right-hand side, such as " Music " or "Dancing." The fashion of late has been to give receptions at which there is no set amusément, and it is correct in such a case to put the word "Conversation." Some hostesses have gone so far as to adopt the negative phraseology and put " No Music," to indicate that the guests must come provided with plenty to say.

In inviting guests to stay in your house, it

is the correct thing, when writing the invitation (which must, of course, be a personal note), to clearly state the length of time you wish them to remain. "Come to dinner, and stay the night." "Come for a week." "We shall expect you for ten days." Some such phrase is easily introduced into your letter, and saves embarrassment on both sides.

In giving a dinner-party, to arrange your guests so that the conversation of the whole table may be agreeable. Nothing is more important—not even the dinner itself—than the bringing together of the right people, who will know how to amuse each other.

While considering the suitability of the party as a whole, to be sure each lady and gentleman will be able to have a fairly agreeable *tête-à-tête* when the conversation is not general; and to remember that when you ask your friends to your table you do so to give them pleasure. Do not ask them at all unless you take the trouble to do this. An unforgiving enemy may be made as readily by careless entertaining as by any other carelessness. You only inflict a hardship on your friend by giving him a bad dinner, or by making him entertain some stupid or unpleasant person during the time taken in consuming a good one.

Whether as host or hostess, to let all your more material anxieties be disposed of satisfactorily beforehand, and to have nothing to think of but the intellectual amusements of your guests. If you are the host, see that the wine is good; that is your one duty at home. Arrange with your wife what standard of excellence you can afford for the dinner, and let her feel that she will have enough money to pay the expense, and a little over, so that there shall be no small economies. Enable her to have everything good of its kind.

To keep out of the house all day when a dinner-party is to be given, so that the servants are fresh for the evening's labours. To be home and dressed, all in easy time, to then look after your special department—the wine—see that the claret is warmed, the sherry ready, and that the right champagne has been brought from the cellar, or supplied you for the evening. Better give your guests lime juice and water than bad wine.

To be perfectly at your ease after this, whatever little accident may happen ; remember that domestic difficulties are soonest forgotten if unnoticed. Devote yourself to your guests, and keep the conversation always alive, while never monopolising it. Let your guests talk, and induce them to do so, it is not your *rôle*.

As the hostess it is the correct thing to free yourself from all small cares beforehand. Be sure of your cook; if you are not, have the dinner sent in. A home-cooked one is best, but there are establishments now in different parts of London which will supply one in good style, and anything is better than a look of anxiety on the hostess's face, or a terrible halt between the courses.

If your dinner is sent in, to allow those who provide it to send waiters, otherwise be sure you can depend on your own resources. Never engage an inexperienced or unknown assistant. One good parlour-maid, who has her reputation at stake, is worth half-a-dozen strange hirelings.

To have the table itself a thing of beauty, decorated according to the latest mode, which changes with every season.

To yourself arrange which lady shall be taken down by which gentleman, and to write the name of each guest on a card placed on the napkin, or perhaps in a cluster of flowers.

To be ready dressed in time to go into the dining room and see that each guest's name is placed correctly, before awaiting the arrivals in the drawing-room.

To indicate to each gentleman, when dinner is served, what lady he takes down.

To see that your guests are amused with each other during dinner, but not to yourself take a conspicuous part in the conversation.

To observe if anyone appears dull or ignored, and address yourself to that person, so that no one is neglected.

AT A DANCE.

It is the correct thing

For host and hostess to devote themselves to their guests, seeing throughout the whole evening that everyone who will dance is supplied with partners.

To see that all your guests in turn visit the supper table. For one young man who knows no one, or one solitary "wall-flower" to pass the evening without dancing and without supper, is the greatest reproach possible to a host or hostess.

Cards are always an alternative for those who do not dance; and sometimes an introduction between two who neither dance or play cards will make the evening pass pleasantly for them. Be sure you let no one sit through the hours unamused. It would be far better not to have invited that person.

To find out all the pretty new figures in the cotillion, and spend a little money on the favours for it; this will always give pleasure.

To have really good music. Whatever else you may have to surrender, to be sure that the wine and the music are good.

AT A RECEPTION.

It is the correct thing

For the hostess to stand in an easily accessible situation (in most London houses the top of the stairway is usually selected, if a large crowd is expected to gather; if the reception is on a small scale, the lady may be reached if she posts herself just inside the drawing-room door), where she remains throughout the whole evening, to greet those who come in and say good-bye to those who go. It is usual to send cards for a reception to the whole of one's visiting list, so that people come and go in numbers, and the hostess has really no other duty but to say "How do you do?" and "Good-bye; so glad to have seen you!" If "Music" is written on her cards, it is correct to have professionals, or at all events to have the programme arranged beforehand, so that she does not leave her post.

For the host to mix among the visitors and talk to them, one after another. Introductions are not expected at receptions, though they may be made.

For people to stand about and talk, not to sit down as if they had come to stay. It is therefore correct to crowd your rooms with visitors, and have most of the furniture removed from it, especially the chairs.

To give a light refreshment in the dining room, supplied by servants; not a supper, but tea, coffee, wine, sandwiches, and cakes.

CHAPTER III.

AS A GUEST—DANCES AND AT HOMES.

<u>It is the correct thing</u>

To arrive within five minutes of the time appointed for lunch or dinner; at a ball or a reception it is best not to appear on the scene for quite an hour after that written on your card, or you may find yourself the only guest.

Never to overstay your welcome, or to run the risk of so doing by staying on when others are leaving, unless you are very specially pressed to do so by your host or hostess.

To decide at once on receiving an invitation whether or no you will accept it, and to reply without delay. Never to commit the *gaucherie* of using a postcard—a liberty only for the very great to take. Your invitation will come on tinted, scented paper, in all probability; let your reply be in as elegant a style.

If you are a dancing man, to remember that you are asked to dances for that reason. It is a very poor compliment to your hostess to stand about in the doorways, instead of helping others to enjoy the evening.

To remember that there is no way of becoming popular better than that of entering into the matter in hand with a will. A dancing man who not only dances with the pretty girls that please his fancy, but can be relied on to lead in the cotillion, and perhaps even to suggest new figures, you will find is always a great favourite.

To take your share of entertaining bores, or people who do not amuse you very much. Your hostess will notice it and be grateful. Pure selfish enjoyment is not always the best policy.

To be quite at your ease with those among

whom you mingle. An unembarrassed manner is a great charm, if it is accompanied by good taste; and if you cannot command this, it is perhaps better to remain in the shade, until you become used to society.

To remember that if you dance often with one young lady you will be understood to be paying her marked attention. Unless you wish this to be implied, be careful to change your partners often, even though one may be more agreeable to you than all the rest.

If you are dancing merely for dancing's sake, and do not wish to monopolise one young lady, to ask some of the wall-flowers or neglected ladies from time to time. You will find this will make you popular with everyone; and very likely you will find the plain girls quite as agreeable companions as the pretty ones, and not so exacting.

To take your partner back to her chaperon after the dance is over, unless you wish to pay her special attention; in which case you can ask her to walk about with you—perhaps even to sit out the next dance—but this will be very marked. In any case it is your duty to take her back eventually to the seat she was in when you asked her to dance, or to her chaperon.

If your partner leaves the house while in your society, to see her downstairs into her carriage and arrange her wraps for her. If you have a previous acquaintance, or are sufficiently encouraged on this occasion, to ask at parting whether you may call the next day and inquire whether she is fatigued. This is a little amusement for the following afternoon which is quite permissible.

To defer to your hostess's wishes as to whom you take down to supper. Of course, if she gives you no hint, you are free to take your partner of the moment; but if she indicates any other arrangement you must fall in with it.

At supper, to wait upon the lady you take down, and see she has all she needs before thinking of your own wants. Where there is not sufficient accommodation for everyone to sit down, the men are not expected to eat until the ladies have had supper, in order to make the arrangements easier. Some gentlemen ignore this custom, but to do so is a mark of ill-breeding.

Nevertheless, it is now more fashionable than it used to be for successive parties of ladies and gentleman to sit or stand at the tables and sup at the same time; and where this is arranged for it is quite correct. At the same time, your partner's wants must be attended to before your own.

It is not correct

For a lady to dance two successive dances with the same partner. If she is a young girl, she can only do this with the man she is engaged to marry.

For a lady to go down to supper alone. She has to wait upon the kindness of her gentlemen friends in these matters, unless she is a belle. One of the agreeable features of the cotillion is the figure in which the ladies choose their partners, thereby for a short time reversing this accustomed order of things.

It is the correct thing

At receptions to give your hostess no trouble, but to find your own acquaintances among her visitors and amuse yourself with them. It is correct at a dance for a man to ask for introductions; if he notices a lady he admires he can ask his hostess to introduce him to her. But this is much more rarely done at receptions, and is not quite the correct thing.

If you are asked to sing, play, or recite, to do so at once or not at all. To make a fuss about it is in the worst possible taste.

To appear to be amused and interested, even if you are not. If you find persons whom you know, to entertain them as much as possible by your conversation. It is your business to be agreeable while in society, and you must remember that the success of a gathering of this kind depends almost entirely on the charm of conversation.

CHAPTER IV.

AS A GUEST—COUNTRY HOUSE VISITING.

It is the correct thing

To arrive on the day specified just in time to dress for dinner, unless you are specially asked to come earlier in the day. To take as little luggage as you conveniently can.

To avoid taking maid, valet, or pet animals, unless asked to do so; strange servants are often as great a trial in a house as strange dogs are.

To avoid, on arrival, fussing about your luggage. A quiet tip to the right person will ensure its appearance in your dressing-room at the right time.

To ascertain, from one of the servants, the

E

usual hours for meals, and conform to them. You will find this make you a favourite with your hostess and her servants. Except in a very large establishment, unpunctuality at meals destroys all comfort; and even in a big house it is only possible to permit breakfast to be a movable feast.

To avoid being too early as well as too late. The servants have their duties to attend to in preparing a meal, and when the gong has sounded, or the hour struck, is the time for those who partake of it to enter the room, not before.

To make yourself useful or agreeable in any way that presents itself, but to avoid intruding on the domestic life of the family more than necessary.

To write, read, or walk in the morning, after breakfast, either alone or with other guests, leaving your host free to attend to his letters or other business, and your hostess to her domestic duties. Of course, if he invite you to accompany him to the stables, or she to

the nursery, that is another matter; but leave
them free to go alone if they wish it.

To keep any extreme views you may hold,
either in religious or social matters, to yourself, unless specially drawn into talking about
them, either by your hostess or with her
approval.

If you are staying with comparative strangers, to conform to their customs on the first
Sunday of your stay. If these do not suit
you, either leave during the week or ascertain
whether your going your own way will cause
any scandal in the household.

To avoid giving unasked advice; repeating
scandal and gossip; commenting on the dress
or manners of other guests; or making any
observation which should lead your hostess
to think you compare your visit unfavourably
with any visit elsewhere. The best way to
produce a favourable impression is to make
people feel pleased with themselves when in
your company. Some persons criticise and
condemn others in order to please those they

are talking to; but this is very dangerous, as these unkind remarks may at any time be repeated.

To be watchful against being in anybody's way, and to exercise tact in this matter.

If your host is receiving a call from an intimate friend, or one who wishes to discuss some business affair, to remember that you have a letter to write or some other important matter to attend to, which will take you out of the room.

When two other guests evidently want a *tête-à-tête*, to adopt a similar plan.

To do so naturally, and without bustle or drawing attention upon yourself.

It is not the correct thing

To put your hosts out of their way in any matter; if you have different tastes from theirs surrender them for the time being.

To arrive in a fluster with a quantity of luggage, and to distract your host with

attending to it. Leave such matters to the
servants, while you go in with your hostess
and take a cup of tea or a glass of sherry, as
coolly as if you were paying an afternoon
call. It is such a mistake to think fussing
about luggage makes it any safer! it only
worries your friends.

To summon servants unnecessarily; to make
them wait on you when they have other duties
to perform; or to make yourself a trial to
them by irregular habits.

To descend in the morning before the shut-
ters are opened and the rooms ready. You
will by that make servants detest you. If
you are an inordinately early riser, write or
read in your own room, out of everybody's
way, or go out of doors, and return at the
breakfast-hour, when everyone else is ready.

To enter into heated arguments, especially
on theology or religion. Such discussions
often destroy friendships.

To take any part in family disagreements.
If such occur in your presence, remain silent,

as an outsider should, and retire as soon as possible.

To take care of "number one" in preference to others. Remember that, as a guest, you occupy a secondary place. If you want to take up all the fire, to sit in the most comfortable armchair, and to have everything your own way, you should stay at home, and not invite any visitors yourself, for if you have these habits you will make but a poor host.

CHAPTER V.

WHEN TRAVELLING.

It is the correct thing

To remember that no duty and no passports are required for good manners, and that they are, therefore, the cheapest and the most useful of travelling companions.

To put one's affairs into satisfactory order before starting on a long journey; for, though travelling has become comparatively safe, accidents may happen, and you will not have your lawyer at hand in case of emergency.

In a sea voyage to remember that sea-sickness developes the ugly traits of the character.

If you cannot resist the *malade de mer*, to go into obscurity, and to avoid unkind criticism of other sufferers.

To remember that the finest preventives of sea-sickness are early rising, a cheerful temper, and careful eating. Early rising (while on board ship) is, perhaps, the most important of the three, as it is the bad air in the body of the vessel which does more to induce sea-sickness than its movements. The resolute traveller who will go early on deck, get an appetite for breakfast and eat it manfully, is pretty sure to be well all day. The first time he stays in his berth in the morning he has succumbed.

To take for granted that the captain and officers of the ship know their duty, and not to commit the *gaucherie* of offering unsolicited advice or making ignorant criticisms.

To remember that the officers are likely to be agreeable, and certain to be influential, friends while you are on the vessel they order; and that chance travelling acquaintances, unaccredited, may prove very dangerous.

To find as much amusement, and to give as much, as possible in the events of the day; this is a preventive for sea-sickness, and an infallible remedy for the *ennui* of travel.

In travelling on the Continent, to remember that the churches and galleries and palaces of the world were not built for the pleasure of tourists; that, on the contrary, tourists are only admitted on sufferance, and as an act of courtesy. Therefore, repay this by courtesy on your own part.

To remember that guide-books often err, and try to get a little first-hand information.

To be as liberal as your means will allow in the matter of fees. Custodians are taught to expect these, and you will benefit by conforming to custom.

To remember that thanks and apologies cost nothing, and indicate good breeding.

To be as careful and correct in dress when abroad as in one's own country. It is a common *gaucherie* among uneducated persons to dress carelessly and vulgarly when in foreign countries. The only result of this is that they make themselves and their own countrypeople despised and laughed at.

To remember that a tourist is none the less a gentleman because he is travelling.

It is not the correct thing

To outrage the manners and customs of the country you are visiting. In Rome you should do as the Romans do ; if you cannot manage this, do not visit them. They do not ask to be insulted by strangers.

To demand luxuries, when travelling in primitive regions, which you cannot have, though doubtless (even if you dwell in a suburban villa) you could have them if you had stayed at home. You did not come out to find these comforts, but other pleasures.

To make yourself an annoyance in any way to a fellow traveller. You may want his kind services before long, and a little courtesy will win a friend on the road.

To imagine that your native tongue is of course not understood by foreigners, and to indulge in free comment in it. Many a traveller has found himself mistaken in this curiously common delusion.

CHAPTER VI.

AT PUBLIC ENTERTAINMENTS.

It is the correct thing

If you take a lady, or escort a party to the theatre or any other public entertainment, to see that the tickets are all right beforehand, and all details arranged, so that there shall be no discussion or difficulties at the doors.

To avoid, by every means in your power, exchanging any hot words with an attendant, supposing any difficulty should arise. Do this if you like when alone, but not if you have a lady under your escort. In this case, pay twice over rather than have any kind of dispute. It is not the correct thing even when alone, but then no one will suffer but yourself. A lady will never forgive you for making her conspicuous.

To pay proper attention to the entertainment you have gone to, even if it fail to please you. It is simply a sign of ill-breeding to talk out loud or evince your *ennui* in any such discourteous way. If the entertainment really fatigues you, it is easy to leave it. In the meantime, you must remember not to disturb others who may possibly be enjoying it; nor to insult the performers, who are but fulfilling their duty.

To express any adverse criticism you may wish to make in a low tone, so as not to be overheard except by your companion. To remember you are not present as a public critic, and other people may like the performance.

To give the necessary "tips" to attendants without ostentation or hesitation. These accustomed charges are known to you beforehand, and it is in very bad taste to make any fuss about them one way or the other.

To ignore any personal acquaintance with the performers, should you chance to possess it, when you are among the audience. The stage and the audience form two separate worlds, and when you go from one to the other you should do so completely.

PART III.

—

The Details of Life.

CHAPTER I.

DRESS AND THE TOILETTE.

It is the correct thing

To be scrupulously particular in matters of the toilette. This is an increasing fashion in society, as we can readily see by the growing number of manicurists and other professional assistants to the toilette. The care of the person cannot be carried to too great an extreme in the present day.

To look upon your morning bath as a duty to yourself and society, and upon spotless linen as of more importance even than good clothes.

Never to be conspicuous in your dressing. Whether man or woman, you can dress in the extreme height of the fashion and yet avoid conspicuousness. Indeed, it is a test of your style being really very good that only the fashionable should be fully able to appreciate it. If it attracts notice from common persons in the street, you may be sure there is something wrong, or that you have gone too far.

To avoid decided colours and large patterns in material; extraordinary shapes or unusual designs in costume. A woman's figure is best shown by a simple gown, and a man's by a well-cut coat of quiet style. But, however subdued your dressing may be, be sure and have coat or gown made by the best tailor or dressmaker that you can possibly afford.

To wear dressing-gown and slippers, even to receive an unexpected visitor in them, in the morning before noon. After that hour a toilette is necessary. This is true for both gentlemen and ladies.

A lady must appear in a walking dress at lunch, whether in her own house or visiting. So must a gentleman. This rule cannot be infringed without discourtesy, the greatest of all social crimes.

A gentleman retains his "walking" or "morning" dress till six or seven o'clock, when he dresses for the evening. But it is quite the correct thing for a lady in her own home, or if staying at another person's house, to take off her short walking-dress in the afternoon and put on a picturesque tea-gown. She can receive visitors in this costume, and more appropriately than in a morning dress.

For a lady to wear this costume at her own dinner-table, or even for an informal dinner party.

For a man always to dress in the evening; if he is alone with his wife, and wishes to be economical, he may wear an old dress coat— but it must *be* a *dress* coat—and he must go to his dressing-room and put on a clean shirt with the same solicitude as if he were going out to dinner.

To remember that these careful daily habits mark the man of true breeding, and preserve an atmosphere in your own home which nothing can replace. If an unexpected visitor comes, there will be nothing to disguise, or conceal, or apologise for. It is the same principle as that of having your tablecloth as spotless, and your silver as bright, however simple your dinner *en famille* may be. An unexpected guest may then be received without dismay.

To remember that evening dress is never appropriate before six in the evening at the earliest, except as an invited guest at the opening of Parliament or some such extraordinary occasion, when special information as to the requisite etiquette should be obtained.

Not to wear jewellery or trinkets in the morning; orders, stars, or crosses, except on State occasions.

To dress very simply in the day-time, though very fashionably.

To dress as brilliantly as means and the occasion will permit at night.

If you are the hostess of a dinner-party, to

dress moderately. It is not good form to eclipse your guests.

As a guest, to be as splendid as you please. It is a compliment to your hostess if you are a little over-dressed ; you may, therefore, safely err on that side.

For a man always to go out in the evening in evening dress, however informally, unless he is specially bidden to a "smoking party." Indeed, if you wish your guests to be conspicuously informal on any occasion, if it is in the evening, it is the correct thing to say in your invitation "Morning dress."

To regard your pocket-handkerchief (when you are in society) as an article of ornament, not of use. The writer once heard this remark made to a beautifully-equipped *mondaine* : "You wear your handkerchief as if it was a bouquet—and it might be one of violets, it is so sweet." The other side of the picture may be conjectured, without description, from the story of a young lady who discarded an accepted suitor because she said he always seemed to have a cold, and made her aware of it even when he was on the doorstep. She had not the courage to look forward to a lifetime of such *gaucheries*. Who can wonder?

It is not correct

To dress in better style than the company you are in, so as to annoy or humiliate its members. To do so is no glory to you, only an indication of ill-breeding.

To wear any jewellery in the morning, except a watch and rings. A woman can wear as many rings as she pleases all through the twenty-four hours if she likes. But if she wears too many it becomes vulgarity, though it is not exactly incorrect. Two or three really valuable ones are sufficient.

To visit friends who are in deep mourning without some deference to their state. It is well, under such circumstances, to dress very quietly, and to avoid all brilliant colourings, if only as a matter of civility.

CHAPTER II.

BREAKFAST—LUNCH—DINNER.

It is the correct thing

If you breakfast in public, to have made a full morning toilette. Bathe, and put on an appropriate dress. A gentleman may appear in a loose coat; a lady in a morning wrapper. If her hair requires elaborate dressing, which cannot be accomplished so early, a coquettish and becoming breakfast cap is distinctly *chic*.

To appear fully equipped, but in a totally different style from that of the evening.

Lend yourself to circumstances as far as possible. If you are asked what you will take, choose what is already on the table, unless it is positively disagreeable to you. Do what you can to avoid giving trouble; it will make you liked by your hostess and by the servants.

If you are in your own house, to be punctual to the appointed breakfast-hour. You expect punctuality from your servants, but you cannot consistently enforce it unless you set the example. Fix the hour yourself, and whether it be eight or twelve adhere to it. Otherwise you set a fatal precedent, and when next you want your early breakfast you will not get it.

AT LUNCHEON.

It is the correct thing

To make a sufficient but a light meal. Do not conduct yourself, whether at home or abroad, as if you were dining, or taking your one heavy meal of the day.

If you are a guest, to arrive punctually to the time named. It is correct to keep accurately to the time for lunch, because the afternoon is supposed to have other engagements, both for yourself and your hostess.

To take your departure within an hour after lunch is over. Coffee is usually served at the table, or immediately on leaving it. Remember that afternoon tea is a separate entertainment, and do not stay for that unless you are specially asked to. Your hostess may have other visitors coming, or may be going out herself.

It is not the correct thing

To be an exacting or troublesome visitor, either at breakfast or luncheon. Be in good time, because these early meals of the day must be quickly disposed of to make room for more important matters. An invitation to lunch means that you are received *en famille*, which is a great compliment, and must be repaid by consideration for the domestic life of the family and its business; invitations to breakfast are more uncommon in this country, though very usual in America. Punctuality is an essential of courtesy in such a case also.

AT DINNER.

It is the correct thing.

To remember that this is the repast *par excellence*—the important meal of the day. To treat it as such in every respect.

To be five minutes late. Literal punctuality is hardly expected, but if you are more than a quarter of an hour late you imply a rudeness to your hostess which no after civility can compensate for. If you wish to inflict an insult on an acquaintance, accept an invitation to dinner and go an hour late, not otherwise.

To wait for your hostess to intimate to you which lady you shall take down to dinner. Then to advance to the lady in question, offer her your arm, and engage her in conversation as agreeably as you can. You should always appear to be pleased with your partner for dinner; you have no means of escaping from the *tête-à-tête*, even if it does not suit you. It is wisest, therefore, to make friends of your hostess, and the lady she has chosen for you, by appearing pleased and making yourself agreeable.

To eat and drink judiciously. There can be no rule laid down as to what is judicious eating and drinking ; but everyone knows what agrees with himself. To remember that you are invited to enjoy a good dinner certainly, but not to gormandise or drink too much. The man who does either forfeits his welcome. Your powers as a conversationalist are wanted late in the evening quite as much as in the early part of it.

It is not correct

To ignore your partner at dinner, however little he or she may be to your taste. Join in the general conversation if you prefer, but address yourself from time to time to your neighbour. This is a duty you owe to your hostess.

To let your hosts see that you have really only come for the sake of eating and drinking.

To forget that if dinner is the important meal of the day in the matters of food and wine, so it is also in courtesy, conversation, and geniality.   It should be a feast for the mind as well as the body.

CHAPTER III.

IN GENERAL.

It is the correct thing

Never to reveal a secret or betray a trust. Treachery is not only a crime, but it is bad form, and will exclude you from society and the confidence of your friends, when you are found out, as you are certain to be sooner or later.

To refuse to listen to gossip about others, especially if a woman's name is mentioned. It is unmanly for a man to allow a woman's reputation to be taken away in his hearing, and in another of her own sex it is contemptible.

To remember that rumour is a lying spirit, and report always untrustworthy.

To live down a scandal about yourself, but never to condescend to contradict it.

To be invariably civil to all dependents and servants. Even if you have reason to correct them, you can do so best by preserving your own dignity.

To be observant, but never to pry into other people's affairs. They do not concern you, and to inquire into them, or talk about them, shows a little mind.

To answer all letters immediately, whether business or personal. It is impolite to delay replying.

To avoid cheap stationery. Buy what is good and fashionable, and have your address stamped on it if you have a permanent one. This saves you a great deal of writing, and ensures your letters being correctly addressed. Niggardliness and false economies are both vices of the worst sort from a social point of view.

To be sure, when you send a present, that the price is not marked on it; and never to send one with the carriage unpaid.

To be kind to children and animals, for the simple reason that anything else is cowardly.

To remember always that speech is silver and silence golden. A thing said cannot be unsaid.

To remember that those who think twice before they speak save themselves many after-regrets.

To avoid personalities. They are a mark of ill-breeding.

To remember that, if you cannot keep your own secrets, it is hardly fair to expect anyone else to keep them for you.

To avoid playing chess, cards, or any other game, unless you can win or lose with equal equanimity and good temper.

To be in time for a train, as you would be punctual for a business appointment. It is a waste of life to miss a train by three minutes, and wait at the station two or three hours for the next.

To live so that when old age comes you will be spared the tortures of remorse and regret.

CHAPTER IV.

AT A WEDDING.

It is the correct thing

For the "breakfast" to be given at the house of the bride's parents or nearest relation.

For prettily printed invitations to be sent to the guests. All good stationers know how to prepare these now, as they are so much used.

To give a champagne breakfast, which is simply an early luncheon, if that is preferred; but it is also quite correct to make the entertaining consist of an "afternoon tea." This does not look so hospitable, but it is, if anything, more fashionable.

If a breakfast is given, to make it as pretty

as possible. More latitude is permissible on an occasion of this kind than at an ordinary party. For instance, it is quite correct to let the guests sit down in small groups at a number of little tables instead of at one large one. When this is done, it is a pretty conceit, which is effective when well carried out, to present every lady and gentleman with flowers to wear of certain colours. Those wearing the same colours go down to breakfast together (the hostess having arranged the parties beforehand carefully, of course) and find the table at which their places are laid by its being decorated with the same flowers and colours. It amuses people to find their partners in this way, instead of being formally assorted by the hostess, and the effect is exceedingly pretty when all are seated.

To give a really good meal, whatever you may decide it to be. If only afternoon tea, let it be hot and good and all it should be. If "breakfast," see that the waiting is as efficient as if you were giving a dinner-party.

Too often the whole household is upset by a wedding, and the breakfast badly served. Guests who have with difficulty obtained a melting ice or a cup of cold tea (as is too often their fate even at smart weddings) will not have the same warm wishes for bride and bridegroom as if they had been properly fed, after giving up their morning to witnessing the ceremony.

For the bride to present the bridesmaids with their dresses. This is not necessary, but it is quite the correct thing.

For the bridegroom to present the bridesmaids with some appropriate trinket, either lockets, rings, or brooches, all being alike and of the same pattern.

It is not the correct thing

To throw rice or old shoes after the married couple when they go away. There is nearly always some boisterous spirit or some old-fashioned person in the company who wishes to do these things. But now that it is not the correct thing for a bride and bridegroom to wear the appearance of being newly married, it is very embarrassing for them to arrive at the station with an old shoe on the top of the carriage, and for the bridegroom to be miserably aware of rice in his pockets.

PART IV.

—

The Studious Part of Life.

CHAPTER I.

IN THE STUDY.

It is the correct thing

All through life to set apart certain fixed hours for study, and to rigidly adhere to them. If you are a business man, and have perhaps only an hour or two to spare for study in the day, you will find great benefit by selecting two especial hours and regarding them as sacredly devoted to that purpose.

To allow nothing to disturb you when in your study. Never permit encroachment on the time given to study, whether it be short or long. Each individual must mark out his hours for himself, according to other occupations, according to constitution, temperament.

and capacity; but it is a rule to be followed by all, that such hours, once chosen, should be sacred. This is only fitting, for it is in these hours that you develop and educate the higher part of yourself. That attention which you give to the appointed time for dinner you can equally well give to the appointed hour for study, and, indeed, as the desire for food for the body at a fixed hour is a matter of habit, so the regular feeding of the mind can become a custom. Indeed, the regularity is more important than the length of time given to study; it is quite possible to study too long, and it is possible to acquire a great deal in half-an-hour's absolute concentration on a subject. It is the habitual daily recurrence of the mind to whatever difficult matter is in hand which gradually gives it the mastery.

To study alone, and avoid working with friends, or with any excuse for conversation. If you are compelled to study in the same room with others, then let absolute silence be the law. There is no other way of preventing minor distractions, and of cultivating the power of concentration which is the first requisite for a student. The working in small classes or clubs has another disadvantage, that it cannot be continued through life, and the man who has worked in this way is at a loss when he finds himself alone, as he must sooner or later. In nothing is self-dependence more important than in study. When death has taken away those we love, when our friends are scattered by circumstances, when age comes and steals our pleasures, then, if we have been in the habit of reading alone, our books are a panacea against the horrors of solitude. Those who live for society and business only, and have never acquired the love of solitary study, lose one of the greatest consolations given to mankind.

To be thorough, precise, and exact in whatever study you have in hand. To remember that, in taking up a new subject, or a fresh language, you are in the position of a general who conquers a country. If he leaves forts

standing in their strength, or districts unsub-
dued, and passes on, he will find that he has to
return and recommence the warfare, or else to
retire discomfited. Want of accuracy frequently makes a man who is really widely
read the laughing-stock of those whose area
of knowledge is much less than his own. This
is bad enough, and the want of confidence in
himself which will follow is much worse still.
He becomes silent, when otherwise he might
lend charm to the conversation, simply
because he is uncertain of his ground. It may
be ignorance of technicalities, or doubt about
the accuracy of a quotation, or an inability (as
with many careless scholars) to speak grammatically, which seals his lips. Any doubt of
his own knowledge is sufficient to silence a
sensitive man, and he will suffer all his life in
consequence, and the worst of it is, the steps
cannot be successfully retraced. The mind
becomes fixed as age advances. It is in youth
that our great opportunities are given us—
opportunities too often wasted for want of

attention to some trifling daily rule, for want of acquiring a correct mental habit.

To regard your efforts in study as profoundly valuable, for they constitute that disciplining of yourself which no one can do for you. Others can give you opportunities, and even assistance, but you cannot be made to learn any more than a horse can be made to drink, even though the water be carried to him. This is what you must do for yourself. It may not be agreeable at first, and, indeed, unless you experience a certain amount of effort, you may feel convinced you are not really accomplishing anything, but merely passing the time.

To remember that in habituating yourself to this sense of effort, and forming the capacity for perseverance, you are attaining a priceless quality, apart from that learning which is the cause of your effort. A shrewd observer of life says, "Great abilities have always been less serviceable to the possessors than moderate ones." This is so true that you will find the faculty of perseverance, which can be acquired by all who are capable of work at all, of more value to yourself than any extraordinary talent would be without it.

To overcome obstacles in the way of an important duty such as study. Do not let trifling engagements or rival interests break in upon your work merely because your hour of study is an engagement with yourself alone. More than that, set yourself to overcome difficulty; to obtain such books as you need, even if they are hard to get, and, if unattainable, to pursue your labour even without them.

CHAPTER II.

IN READING.

It is the correct thing

To remember that one's library is an index to one's character.

To remember that a taste for good reading can be cultivated.

To remember that a few books well studied are more beneficial than a great many carelessly read.

To consider money spent on good books as money well invested.

To adopt a certain system in reading. If a particular subject interests you, study one author after another upon it, so as to get an intelligent view of the matter, not a partial, one-sided one. You will find this plan of great benefit, and very interesting.

To remember that there are books of all kinds, representing every phase of the human mind, and that one reads for different purposes at different times.

To remember that, though no one could read through all the good books that have been written in the course of the longest life, yet, by devoting a certain fixed time to real study every day, a great many good books can be mastered.

To know that reading for relaxation and amusement is entirely different from study.

To know that fiction is one of the best forms of relaxation; it is only the narrow-minded who affect to disdain it. The great Cardinal Newman delighted in a good novel, and the names of many great men might be given who also habitually read fiction for relaxation and profit.

To realise that nothing enervates and weakens the powers of the mind more readily than the constant reading of trashy and foolish literature.

To remember that the good and clever magazines of the day, though ephemeral, represent the passing thought and feeling of intelligent persons, and should therefore be read from time to time. This will be found a great assistance in conversation.

For parents to recollect that books are a powerful educational agency, and actually form the bent of the mind. What children read is never forgotten.

To remember that there are books which blight and destroy the mind and soul, as there are books which feed and strengthen. As in feeding the body, so in feeding the intellect: there is bread and wine, or there is poison. This is true of all kinds of books, but it perhaps is specially true of poetry and fiction. The despair which breathes all through Byron's poems must affect the student who enters fully into them. Byron, being the master of modern English poetry, and an example in the use of the language, must be read, and read appreciatively, by a student of poetry, but it is well to take an antidote, as we do in matters of food. Byron is too strong meat without some tempering salad.

To remember that the mind is plastic. If you allow it to take on the form of despair, you will regret it afterwards, for desperate thoughts are not agreeable ones.

To remember that this applies to all bad books. Beware of them. If you are not afraid of becoming demoralised, then beware of becoming wretched, a state all men dread, and it is as easily induced by bad reading as by bad companions.

To remember that a book can be tasted, like wine. If you find that a glass of wine out of a fresh bottle has a wrong flavour about it, you do not drink off the whole bottle in order to ascertain positively that it is not good! No, you have too much respect for your health. Respect your health of mind in the same way, and you will intuitively form a good library.

To know that books are in reality the fountain of knowledge. Your mode and style of thought and speech will be formed on what you read.

To recollect that it is better to read a little and thoroughly than to skim through many books. Even in fiction, if a romance is written by a good author who is an observer of life, it will repay being read slowly, and re-reading. Do not read too many books! It is probable that the ancients were gainers rather than losers from possessing so few books. The necessity for thorough study strengthened the mental powers.

It is not the correct thing

To ape any tastes you do not possess. Let the books on your shelves be the books you read, and if you have well-worn copies of volumes that you have read a dozen times, preserve these as you would old friends. They do you honour.

H

To forget that a man or woman of the world can judge your character by a glance round your library shelves.

To forget that it is useless to affect a learning you have not got; a few moments' conversation will show an intelligent person whether your mind is reflected in the furniture of these shelves or not.

To read any and everything carelessly. Let the principle of selection be shown, even in the magazines and papers that lie on your table.

CHAPTER III.

IN WRITING.

It is the correct thing

To be careful, even to fastidiousness, in respect to handwriting, for nothing shows a man or woman's character more plainly. It is a noticeable fact that authors, who write a great deal, often acquire a delicate and beautiful handwriting, while ladies of fashion, careful and dainty in other matters, write an untidy, careless hand. This is partly from lack of interest in the matter. Certainly the handwriting indicates character, and cannot be entirely changed; but it can be greatly improved by care and attention. The best

possible method of acquiring a good formation of the individual letters is to take the
Greek alphabet and copy it out carefully
every day. This soon effects a wonderful
improvement.

To remember that in ordinary correspondence, even in writing mere notes, a good style
is very important. When you look over your
letters on the breakfast table you will notice
that you take up some with more pleasure
than others, even if from the same class of
people. A pretty or tasteful paper; a charac-
teristic handwriting; even an agreeable per-
fume, if not too strong—these things attract
you. But if you hold two notes in your hand,
and you know from experience that one con-
tains curt sentences, and information given in
the barest words, and that the other, however
brief, will have a *bon mot* introduced which
will make you smile, and a charming word of
friendship or courtesy at the close, will it
not be the latter that you will open first?
Remember this when you are writing notes

yourself; it is possible to write them so that they will always be welcomed.

With the penny post, and the facilities it affords for perpetual communication, the art of correspondence is supposed to have died out; but, as a matter of fact, it has simply changed its character. It was once a serious art, now it is a trifling one. But, nevertheless, it *is* an art. No one writes letters now; even in corresponding from one side of the world to the other a note is sufficient—sometimes even a postcard. But that does not alter the fact that in these slight missives you create things permanent, which are a record of yourself. The little note of friendship can bear upon it an indication of real feeling, even in a few words; the badinage in a mere line exchanged between acquaintances can be agreeable and well-chosen, or the reverse.

To remember that when you have posted your letter it is no longer your property. It has gone out to the world; you can never get it back. It has been decided by the law that while the paper your letter is written on belongs to your correspondent (which prevents your asking for it back, or attempting to regain possession of it), the matter of the letter belongs to yourself (this making it impossible for your letters to be published without your consent). But while you cannot get your letter back, your correspondent may show it to whomsoever he will; therefore, never be careless in letter-writing.

To sleep on a decision or a fit of anger when either have to be communicated by letter. This gives you an immense advantage, which you lose if your communication is verbal. Don't waste this advantage by posting your letter in a hurry. Especially in cases of anger observe this rule. It is wonderful what foolish things we all say when we are angry! Write your letter—relieve yourself of your rage—then put the letter by till the next morning, and read it again. In one instance out of ten you will think it fits the circumstance, and post it; in the others you will probably throw it into the fire and laugh at yourself—thanking your prudence, meantime, that it is you who laugh, and not your correspondent.

To be careful, when you are writing a letter of any importance, that your words and phrases will convey the meaning you intend them to. If possible, submit your letter to a third person, to ascertain that this is so. Terrible misunderstandings and misfortunes have arisen before now from using a phrase capable of two interpretations.

CHAPTER IV.

IN EDUCATION.

It is the correct thing

For parents to educate their children very carefully.

To remember that one's own education is never completed.

To remember that a true education must be physical, mental, and spiritual.

To understand that true education is the perfecting, completing, training, and developing of all one's powers.

To remember that a little learning is a dangerous thing, and that if a subject is touched at all it should be studied thoroughly.

To favour that system of education which produces good citizens and good members of the family.

To recollect that children, while still children, belong to their parents, who alone are responsible for the education which shall make them good or bad citizens, sons or daughters, later on.

To know that education does not merely mean the filling of the mind with information or a collection of facts, however well ordered these may be.

To remember that a child has to learn to think and act for himself by degrees, else he will have no independence of action when he becomes a man. The development of the reasoning faculty is one of the most important results of a right education, and the power of independent decision must be developed with it. Over-education in mere learning frequently weakens these powers, and makes a man useless in the practical affairs of life.

To know that the formation of the judgment

is a vital part of education. To enter upon life full of accomplishments, and with a highly cultivated mind, but without the judgment formed, is like entering an arena unarmed, without any weapon of defence. The habit of weighing and balancing opinions and theories, which can be acquired during education, prepares the mind to consider courses of action in the same manner, and also to judge of others by their conduct and circumstances. When the judgment is untrained, the last book read is the most wonderful, the newest theory the truest, the latest acquaintance the most valuable.

To remember that much of the mere task-work of education has a greater result than the acquirement of a particular form of detail knowledge—it induces the virtue of patience. Once having commenced a tedious study, never allow yourself to throw it aside until accomplished (or unless something more important claims your attention). To throw it aside because it is tedious is to commence a fatal habit which will prove your own destruction later in life.

To recollect that the memory, which is continually in use during education, is one of your most important faculties. Train it steadily, as you would a restive horse, and you will have a servant whose value cannot be over-rated. Perhaps, in this respect, it is left for those of defective education to realise what they have lost, and which they must miss as long as they live. It is for this reason that you should never permit the tediousness of a lesson that has to be learned by rote to conquer your patience.

It is not the correct thing

To allow a child to see different manners and customs out of lesson hours from those which its teachers inculcate, and then to blame it for adopting them.

To forget that *everything* you teach your child is part of its education ; from the moment it opens its eyes till it becomes a man or woman it is learning. If, for instance, the child sees you do not always adhere to the truth, can you doubt but your influence will be as strong as the teacher's, who tells it that falsehood is a sin?

To imagine that education consists of passing through certain courses and routines, and learning certain lessons by rote.

To forget that the whole of life is one long education.

To imagine that your children will not reward you later on for all the good you teach them, and to forget that all carelessness will bring its fruit also.

To acquire any knowledge, whether of a subject or a language, partially or imperfectly. Whatever you do, do thoroughly, and then you will always be able to hold your own among others.

THE FINE ARTS.

It is the correct thing

To give some intelligent study to the arts, even if you have no especial taste for them. A man who is an eminent classical scholar or mathematician, and never cares to look at a picture or listen to a sonata, is developed all on one side, and is a species of monster. Great minds are intensely appreciative, and though they excel but in one form of effort, know enough of all others to learn by and benefit from the genius of other men. The tendency to live in one groove of thought is common among mediocre persons simply because it is easy. A really well-educated and cultivated man should exhibit the same comprehensive spirit as the man who is greatly gifted by nature.

To remember that a visit to the Royal Academy or the New Gallery on a crowded day, and an unintelligent contemplation of the results of a year of modern work, does

not constitute an education in art. Even if
you do not care for pictures, it is well to go
to the old masters and fix your attention upon
them; at least, learn their names, note what
schools they belong to, and study their
manner of working as intelligently as you
can. If possible, gather some of their glory
to yourself, and let it enlarge your mind.

To be able to speak with some knowledge of
pictures. It is not necessary to have a special
taste for art in order to appreciate it. If you
do not take some trouble in cultivating yourself in this way, you will regret it very much
some day, when art is being spoken of and you
find yourself ignorant of its simplest language.
Our great public galleries and museums make
art as accessible as literature, and it lies
entirely with the student himself to decide
whether he shall know anything on the
subject or not.

To be modest in respect to what you may
know on such subjects. You need to be able
to understand and take part in a discussion,

not to exhibit the fact that you have acquired a little superficial knowledge, or had some special opportunities.

To use every opportunity which comes in your way of such mental education. When you travel find out what public galleries there are in the cities you visit, and remember that every moment spent in them intelligently is of the greatest value in your education. All through your life this form of cultivation can be continued and enlarged, and in later years you will be glad indeed that you have attuned your mind to such studies. For sometimes a taste which is not inborn can be developed, and become a gratification of the best sort. Many a business man, when he has retired from the active part of his life, becomes a collector, whose time and money is not only a source of pleasure and profit to himself, but of value to the world. This cannot be, however, if in his earlier years he permits himself to remain profoundly ignorant of all those interests with which he is not specially concerned.

To remember that even a slight knowledge of painting and sculpture, if it is accurate, will often be the means of giving pleasure to others, and is of social value. This, not merely in conversation, but by being able to act as cicerone and guide when you meet your friends abroad. Nothing is more painful than the position of an uncultivated and unintelligent tourist in some historic city, when he meets cultivated people of his acquaintance. He finds himself an " outsider," and this merely for want of a little patient effort and research.

To know that what has been said of painting and sculpture is true also of music. To be "musical" is one thing; to be able to understand and appreciate music is another. An occasional attendance at popular concerts will enable the student to discriminate between different kinds of music. No matter, however little natural ear one may possess, it is possible to know a sonata of Beethoven's or a waltz of Chopin's.

It is not the correct thing

To suppose that to study the fine arts means the attempt to produce. This is a common mistake. It is no more a part of artistic education than is it the business of a student of literature to write a book. Doubtless, the student will write exercises ; but he does not expect his friends to read them. Why, then, should he exhibit his amateur sketches, or propose to sing or play? Such powers are special gifts, and not to be discovered in every student.

To run the risk of boring any social circle by an exhibition of your amateur powers. That is not the way to show your education in art.

I

PART V.

—

The Formation of Habit.

CHAPTER I.

IN DAILY LIFE.

It is the correct thing

To live a straightforward and upright life, orderly and decent in everything. This can only be done by the formation of habits.

To remember that a habit is as easily cultivated or reared as a plant or an animal. Daily attention is absolutely essential for success in any of these instances, and if it is given then success is certain. Without it, of course, nothing can be done.

To know that any taste or inclination can be overcome by this method. Resistance, if persevered in without wavering, will alter the strongest tendencies.

To know that a thing which is at first positively repugnant will eventually become desired and agreeable by dint of systematic repetition.

To remember that if children are allowed to spend money, and taught to spend it economically, the habit will cling to them throughout life.

To know that with yourself, if you have not been trained in this way when young by others, the habit of using money rightly can be aquired by systematic effort.

Never, whether you are rich or poor, to allow yourself to owe any man anything. What you cannot afford to buy, do without. This is entirely a matter of habit, and those who fail to form the habit not only injure others, but lay up a store of unhappiness for themselves. There must come an end to the pleasure of gratifying every caprice; if from no other cause, from satiety, the saddest of all causes.

To remember that habits of industry are quite easily acquired by resolution, and that there is no excuse for the man who does not form them.   To rich or poor they are essential if anything is to be accomplished during life. A rich man without these habits sinks into obscurity.

To know that early rising is valuable, not merely because it counteracts the tendency to mere sloth, and enables you to use the best hours of the day for work or study, but also because it prevents that midnight dissipation which is fatal when it becomes habitual.

To accustom yourself to fulfil your intentions and resolves.   Never break a promise you have made to yourself.   To do so is the surest way of losing your self-respect.   If you have determined to rise early, do not let idleness break your determination when the time comes.   If you have made certain plans for the day, resolutely carry them out.   It is a good plan, and one adopted by many eminent and successful men, to note down what has to be done in the day, and to regard it as a sacred duty that these notes shall all be marked off "done."   This custom strengthens the character, and may with advantage be adopted by all, from the student to the millionaire, who has simply engagements to keep. Some persons' lives are of so simple a nature that it is unnecessary to make notes, but it is sufficient if they resolve to execute a certain amount of work, or make a particular effort. In that case all that is needed is unflinchingly to adhere to the amount resolved upon, and not permit any excuse to induce you to leave off before. If you have attempted too much, set a smaller task for the next day; but, whatever you do, do not break faith with yourself. In later life men will pay you the tribute of saying, " He promised, and he is sure to perform," because you will have made it a second nature always to fulfil your intentions. Many persons leave promises unfulfilled from the sheer habit of forgetfulness, not at all from intention, and, in consequence, they lose their friends and are avoided; for there is nothing which sooner makes a man isolated than being found unreliable.

CHAPTER II.

IN MATTERS OF BUSINESS.

It is the correct thing

For a man who has no profession and no occupation, nevertheless, to be as exact and punctual in business matters as those whose lives are devoted to it.

Never to neglect the business matters in connection with your affairs. To do so means, too probably, ruin at some future day, and certainly embarrassment.

For a rich man to understand the value of money just as well as a poor one.

To recollect that there is nothing grand in being cheated or in throwing money away by

unbusinesslike proceedings. Those who benefit by it only ridicule you. If you have money
to waste, there are always a hundred persons
at hand who are in real need and can be benefited by it.

While young, it is the correct thing to listen
to the wisdom of those who are older and more
experienced, in matters of business. For business has to be learned; it takes time and
practice. The young man who thinks he
knows better than his elders in this respect
often regrets his folly for life. The most
experienced person you can meet with is your
best adviser on business matters.

To observe the habits of successful men and
endeavour to acquire them. You will find
they are careful, watchful, prompt, exact.

In business you cannot act in a hurry, you
cannot pass over trifles as if of no importance,
you cannot be dilatory or careless.

To accustom yourself to attend to and reply
to a business communication immediately.
Never to throw it aside while you entertain

yourself more agreeably. No one can afford to do this, not the richest man in the world. If he allows himself to do so, some day there is an end to his riches and his pleasure.

To answer all business letters promptly, even if they do not immediately interest you or concern yourself. You will find the more eminent and successful a man is, the more strictly this rule is adhered to.

To be methodical with all your papers, and to keep all receipts and all documents carefully and in order. If you make this a habit you will find it of infinite value as you go through life.

These things are of importance to yourself, and it lies with yourself to take care of them, and to have right on your side when you need it. The prosperity of a life has been wrecked before now for the want of this simple habit, which is very easily formed. And, in smaller matters, it is only a careless and foolish person who is compelled to pay a bill twice over for want of having kept a receipt. Careful business habits are of the greatest use in all matters, great or small, throughout life.

To keep copies of all important letters that you write, and retain them.

To check your expenditure by simple and practical rules, which will always suffice to keep you out of momentary troubles. The first of these is, spend always a little less than you have, whether it be a million or a shilling; any other course brings heart-breaking consequences.

CHAPTER III.

IN MATTERS OF TASTE.

It is the correct thing

To exhibit good taste; and this, when not intuitive, as it is in some cases, is a matter of habit.

Many persons are without intuitive taste, and are, therefore, obliged to follow the lead of others. If you are in this position, or if you are easily influenced by others, be sure that you choose good models; for you will soon acquire their tastes, and learn to like what pleases them; your faculties will become attuned to theirs. This is entirely a matter of habit, if there are no very strong natural proclivities.

To observe, when you hear a person spoken of as possessing excellent taste, in what way they exhibit this, and endeavour to acquire the same. From a minor detail, such as dress, to the great one of the fine arts, you will find that habit will change your desires. In wine and in food it is necessary for the palate to be habituated with what is good before it can become critical. So with music, painting, literature; so with manners, customs, modes of life.

To aim, therefore, at the highest standard you can find, in order to acquire habits and tastes of the best kind possible to you. In this way these will become natural, and you will form a good taste of your own.

To pay attention to good criticism, and to listen to the opinions of those who understand the subjects of which they talk.

To endeavour to follow them in their appreciation; not merely to imitate, but to discover what it is that they admire, and learn to obtain the same refined pleasure yourself if possible. It is in this way that you will acquire the habit of good taste.

CHAPTER IV.

IN QUESTIONS OF INDULGENCE.

<u>It is the correct thing</u>

To have your desire for pleasure under control, not to yield to it, like a child or an animal, without reason.

To remember that every indulgence brings with it its punishment, and you cannot take it without also accepting its consequences. There is no evading this law of nature, which is inexorable as nature itself.

To know that, even in the smallest matter, this same rule holds good. The apparently trivial matters of diet, of stimulating drinks, of idleness, are of vital importance in reality,

as they involve life-long consequences, which
can never be escaped from.

To remember, therefore, that, when you
form good habits in these matters, you are
being your own best friend. Frugality,
abstemiousness, moderation in all appetites,
industriousness, and activity, are much more
matters of habit than people ordinarily suppose. Once acquired, they become agreeable,
and the result conduces to a successful and
healthy life.

CHAPTER V.

THE CHOICE OF FRIENDS.

It is the correct thing

To be very careful in choosing one's friends; and to prefer friends who will benefit you to those who will not. Never forget the rule which Mason gives, "Choose your company for profit, just as you do your books." This is as much a matter of habit as anything else.

To acquire the habit of associating with those who are your superiors in intelligence and education. In this way you will always gain by contact with your friends. Moreover, you will also habituate yourself to modesty, which will make you a much more agreeable companion.

To accustom yourself to seek out those who

have special qualities and gifts, and endeavour to absorb into your mind some of their *esprit*. In this manner you will acquire a cultivated habit in thought and feeling.

To value persons not according to the wealth or position, which has come to them by accident, but by the respect in which they are held. The habit of associating with those who are highly esteemed will win you respect also.

No better conclusion could be made to this chapter on habit than to quote a few of the seventy resolutions of President Edwards, who built up a noble life by setting himself the daily task of living nobly :—

" Resolved, never to do any manner of thing, whether in soul or body, less or more, but what tends to the glory of God, nor *be*, nor *suffer* it, if I can possibly avoid it.

"Resolved, never to lose one moment of time, but to improve it in the most profitable way I can.

" Resolved, to live with all my might while I do live.

"Resolved, never to do anything which I should be afraid to do if it were the last hour of my life.

"Resolved, to maintain the strictest temperance in eating and drinking.

"Resolved, never to do anything which, if I should see it in another, I should count a just occasion to despise him for, or to think any the more meanly of him.

"Resolved, never to speak anything but the pure and simple verity.

"Resolved, never to allow the least measure of any fretting or uneasiness at my father or mother. Resolved to suffer no effects of it, so much as in the least alteration of speech, or motion of my eye, and to be especially careful of it with respect to any of our family."

PART VI.

——

The Heart and Conscience.

CHAPTER I.—*The Motives of Life.*

CHAPTER I.

THE MOTIVES OF LIFE.

It is the correct thing

To have an assured motive in life, a certain goal to be attained, or at all events aimed at. Without this life is meaningless, and is too likely to become degraded. In reading biography and history it will be seen that men who have attained eminence have during life gazed on and up at a high and difficult goal.

The motives of life which animate our actions may be summed up under four heads —pleasure, wealth, the applause or admiration of others, or genuine benevolence.

It is scarcely necessary to dwell upon the

consequences of taking the first object as the life-motive. The man who does so simply throws away his career and his opportunities, for he is absolutely certain to become the slave of his passions. Pleasure is necessary in its place, but it must be a subject. Directly the desire for it obtains the mastery, the man is lost. The pursuit of wealth is less injurious and degrading than the pursuit of pleasure, chiefly because it is not enervating. It requires all the faculties trained and the intelligence awake. A man cannot pursue wealth and be slothful or careless, but he can be mean, avaricious, unscrupulous—very different vices, but equally bad. Therefore, wealth, though it is a desirable object, is not worthy to be the life-motive. Nothing which lowers a man's character should hold that place. The desire for the approval of the world is a loftier aim than either of these, and will often bring out all a man's strength and develop the power of his intellect. But nothing brings more acute and bitter, and often undeserved, disappointments than ambition. Its rewards are uncertain, for the world is capricious, and treats its favourites with careless indifference if they fall but ever so little in favour. An ambitious man will unexpectedly find himself deposed, and what resource has he? None, for he has become, in the course of his pursuit, a sublime egotist, utterly selfish. For him there is but one person in the universe, and that is himself. When that person fails him he is disappointed indeed!

The correct standard is one which will not fail you after the first heat of life is over, and leave you without a hope or a solace. The only motive which will make a life rich and powerful from beginning to end is that of benevolence.

To cultivate the heart as earnestly as the intellect, and similar methods can be used in its development.

To remember that the heart is as hard to subdue as the mind. The effort of persevering study disciplines the mind. By attention the heart can in an analogous manner be guided aright.

To know that to allow yourself to become selfish is to allow yourself to become contemptible. You will lose all your friends, for no one likes a selfish person, and it is impossible for him to be loved.

To check your selfish instincts; learn to think of others and of their interests, and try to feel more pleasure when you have benefited another than when you have benefited yourself. This will become easy and natural to you in time, and will endear you to your friends. You will be amply rewarded in the end, for there will come a time when you will yourself need help and sympathy, and will be glad to lean on the friends you have gathered round you.

To check your heart in its wilful impulses, which are often utterly misguiding. Weigh what you do if you wish to act rightly. The impetuousness of feeling will sometimes lead you to be generous before you are just; perhaps, let us say, to give away money which you owe. This is both a folly and a wrong.

To make your conscience the arbiter in such matters The heart should not act alone.

To listen to your conscience, and by constant attention to its voice to help it to become strong. An eminent author observes that no man ever became intemperate or profane at once; that he cannot become a proficient in any sin by a single leap. This is perfectly true. The conscience has to be hushed day after day, till at length it is silent, before proficiency can be attained.

To remember that it is the conscience that lifts man above the level of the animals, and if you would be noble, loved, and respected, cultivate it and listen to it constantly.

To know that the approval of your own conscience is what you need, in preference to any applause or admiration from your fellow-men. They can never judge your motives for action, or know your heart as you can yourself.

It is for you to decide whether what you do is good or bad. Reject the bad unflinchingly, and do what you know is good, and you will create that noble life which is the one lofty aim.

To remember that by this method you secure to yourself the utmost amount of happiness in the end, for all lesser aims involve incessant disappointments.

PART VII.

Conversation.

CHAPTER I.

IN SPEECH.

It is the correct thing

To speak grammatically. Study books of grammar, and read the works of good authors, with a view of learning how to form your sentences. Nothing shows want of education so much as incorrect grammar. If you want to affect the slang of the day *(which is very bad taste)*, do so upon a basis of good speech, or else you only appear ignorant.

To attend to the pronunciation of persons you know to be cultivated, and carefully imitate them. In some cases, a mispronunciation is a species of slang; but be sure you know what you are doing when you adopt such methods of speaking, or you may be laughed at instead of laughed with.

To remember that, according to Thackeray, some slang is gentlemanly and some vulgar; but, as it is very hard to know which is which, it is wiser to err on the right side, and use as little as possible.

To remember that to show respect to your elders and superiors in speech is the correct thing. But it must be done with intelligence. It is old-fashioned and provincial now for one gentleman to use "sir" in speaking to another of the same standing. Everyone uses this term of respect in addressing the Prince of Wales; every young man who knows what is correct uses it in addressing his father or his tutor, but in any other circumstances it is out of place. The corresponding term, "Madam," or "Ma'am," has passed out entirely, and is now used only by servants; the same is true of "Miss." The full surname must always be used in addressing a lady.

To remember that to clip your words, or disfigure them, is only a sign of ill-breeding, not of smartness.

To remember that one great use of the stage is, that you may learn from it how to speak. If you frequent high-class performances, you will become habituated to good pronunciation and imperceptibly acquire the rules of elocution.

It is not the correct thing

To catch up phrases or mannerisms from your inferiors. This habit will cause you to blush for yourself some day, if you acquire it. If you are often with your groom, let him learn to speak from you, not you from him.

To speak a foreign language before a person who does not understand it. There is no surer sign of ill-breeding than to exclude any single member of a company from the conversation in this way. If, at a dinner-table where a

L

dozen are seated, one person does not understand French, or Italian, the others will avoid using those languages, and that without indicating in any way their reason for doing so.

To exhibit your learning by quoting scraps of Latin or Greek, or any other language you may have at command, unless those with whom you are in company are equally scholarly, and certain to understand your allusions.

CHAPTER II.

CONVERSATION IN GENERAL.

It is the correct thing

When a more eminent authority has already expressed perfectly what has to be said on any particular subject, to acknowledge it; and I cannot do better, in opening this chapter, than illustrate this rule by quoting a few of Mason's axioms with regard to conversation. One of his best I will place first:—

"If you can receive neither improvement nor entertainment from your company, furnish one or both for them. If you can neither receive nor bestow benefit, leave that company at once.

"Study the character of your company. If they are your superiors, ask them questions, and be an attentive hearer; if your inferiors, do them good.

"When the conversation droops, revive it by introducing some topic so general that all can say something upon it.

"Never be a cipher in company. Try to please, and you will find something to say that will be acceptable. It is ill-manners to be silent.

"Join in no hurry and clamour.

"Never repeat a good thing in the same company twice.

"Do not affect to shine in conversation, as if that were your peculiar excellency and you were conscious of superior ability.

"Bear with much that seems impertinent. It may not appear so to all, and you may learn something from it.

"Be free and easy, and try to make all the rest feel so. In this way much valuable thought may be drawn out."

Here, perhaps, as well as anywhere may be placed the golden rule, *"Watch your temper!"* and yet this should, in reality, be repeated throughout the whole code of conduct; but, in society, to lose one's temper means to lose all. Argument or discussion become impossible; social intercourse is restricted to the merest superficialities for fear of unfortunate results from the introduction of any more interesting topics. This will be very unfortunate for you, as you may derive great benefit from hearing different views about any subject.

To remember that, however convinced you may be that your own view is right, it is always possible that you may be mistaken, and in social conversation you must always adopt the position that you may possibly not be right, and bring forward what you have to say modestly, and, if possible, with some good proofs. This will produce a valuable effect, and if the subject under discussion is an important one, you will have done some good; whereas, if you lose your temper, you only weaken your cause, for no one cares to listen to a dogmatist.

To know that good humour, or the habit of being easily pleased, is an essential part of politeness, and, therefore, most necessary in conversation.

To remember that cheerfulness, even gaiety, can be cultivated, and it is the quality which will make you welcome in society above all others. If, when you enter a room, you perceptibly brighten the conversation without monopolising it, or in any way becoming obtrusive, you will always be welcomed, both in the home circle and in society in general.

To bear in mind that to see faces light up with pleasure at your entrance will bring you far more satisfaction than any selfish talk of yourself or indulgence in melancholy brooding ever can. Therefore, aim to obtain this. And here I must quote a very telling sentence from another author :—

" There is no real life but cheerful life ;

therefore valetudinarians should be sworn, before they enter into company, not to say a word of themselves until the meeting breaks up."

This may be said not only of valetudinarians, but of all persons who think more of themselves than of anyone else, or whose minds run in one narrow groove only. It is a certain fact that ill-health, suffering, or trouble will not prevent a man from lending brightness to any circle he may join, if he understands the art of conversation, and knows correctly the duties of social intercourse.

CHAPTER III.

CONCERNING STORIES AND ANECDOTES AS PART OF CONVERSATION.

It is the correct thing

To amuse and interest those with whom you are talking, not to bore or weary them, and no part of conversation may be more effectually used for either purpose than the telling of stories and anecdotes.

To be sure, when you tell a story, that there is no one among the company who has heard you tell it before. If there is, the *ennui* experienced by that one person will slightly affect all present.

To remember that the great danger to a successful *raconteur*, and the way in which sooner or later he usually loses his popularity, is that of repetition. Like most other things, the telling of stories is a matter of habit ; and some men, who get the reputation early in life of being good story-tellers, become later on bores from whom everyone flies, simply because they have acquired a chronic habit of relating well-worn anecdotes. It is impossible for any chronic story-teller to have new stories to give his hearers continually, consequently he imperceptibly adopts the story-teller's habit of going through a series—when it is finished it is recommenced ; and though when you first meet a person of this kind you find them delightful company, and their fund of anecdotes seems inexhaustible, in a little while you, like the rest of his old friends, begin to dread meeting him, least you should be expected again to laugh at some old history you have already laughed at a dozen times. If you do not wish yourself ever to be regarded in this way, be sure you do not acquire the reputation of a story-teller.

To remember that, in conversation, an

anecdote should never be told for its own sake, but simply to illustrate a subject which is being talked about. A story that is dragged in is never appreciated; but if it is apt to the moment, it will always be appreciated, as it breaks up and brightens the conversation.

To be careful, if you are telling of a circumstance which has happened to yourself, not to embellish or alter it in any way. Some men, in their desire to shine as story-tellers, allow themselves so to embellish and alter facts in their narration of them that eventually they lose the habit of truth, and no one believes what they say.

PART VIII.

—

Out-of-Door Life.

CHAPTER I.

WALKING—GAMES.

It is the correct thing

To regard exercise as a duty, a physical virtue, never to be neglected.

To remember that, if you do not systematically exercise the body, you will be rewarded by premature old age. When others are in the prime of life, you will have lost all taste for its pleasures, all capacity for its duties.

To remember that, however great a rider or driver you may be, you must not lose the habit of walking. It is necessary for the health to walk regularly. Because you do not feel the necessity for this exercise, do not omit it; you will bitterly regret it later on if you do.

To remember that the habit of walking gives you pleasures all your own, and which are entirely independent of extraneous aids. A man who has learned to be fond of walking is richer than the man with the finest stables in the world. There are well-known and eminent men, good riders and drivers, with plenty of horses at command, who are to be seen every day taking long walks alone, either in town or country.

To remember that in walking one sees the world quite differently from the view one obtains of it in a carriage or on horseback; and the mind can be used intelligently and delightfully by a pedestrian as well as the body. The correct carriage in walking is more easily obtained by a man who fences and takes a certain amount of gymnastic exercise than by any other. The body should be held upright, and the whole of it move slightly with the action of walking, but be very careful that you do not walk with the arms and shoulders. This is a fault even more common with ladies than with men, and produces a most ungraceful carriage. Learn to walk freely and easily, but without any unnecessary swing.

To remember that all games, such as fencing, boxing, &c., and all gymnastic exercises (if not carried to excess), increase both the grace of the movements and the health of the body. Therefore it is correct to neglect no opportunity of learning these under the best masters you can obtain. This is true for both sexes. Fencing has become fashionable with ladies now, and it certainly adds much to their grace in walking or dancing.

To take an interest in becoming proficient in all out-of-door games : they add a pleasure to life, both for yourself and others, and are distinctly beneficial to the health.

CHAPTER III.

DRIVING.

It is the correct thing

Even if you do not drive yourself, but merely ride in your carriage, to know how the carriage and horses should be kept, and show an interest in the subject, otherwise your servants are sure to neglect their duty. Some men simply get into the carriage at the last moment, and drive away without a glance at its condition or at the horses. Persons of this sort would do well to hire both carriage and horses, as they will be cheated less.

by it; he can tell by the feel of his horse if he contemplates doing anything out of the common, and can nearly always forestall him without the horse seeming to be aware of it. He is always carried well and pleasantly."

Never to forget these words, written by a great authority on horsemanship.

Never to forget that a bully is a bad rider, spoils his horse, and loses the respect of good horsemen.

In learning to ride, to learn to understand your horse, as well as to learn how to make him understand you.

To remember that the first requisite, the absolute essential, is a firm seat.

To remember that a strong seat is not necessarily a good one. There are men who cannot be thrown, with nerves like steel, and a seat strong enough to hold on under all circumstances, yet who are not good riders. Such men are never given the best mounts in their friends' stables.

To know that the chief point in acquiring a

M

good seat is to learn to sit in the right place, right in the middle of the saddle. Some men always sit too far back, and sit firmly in that position from long practice; but to do so prevents their ever being able to use their legs properly, which is a great loss. Robert Weir gives a very clear description of a good seat, which I cannot do better than quote :—

"The man who has good hands and seat— and they go very much together—is he who sits well down in the middle of his saddle in an easy, natural position, the upper part of his body over his hips, or, if inclined either way, a little back; his thigh well down the flap of the saddle, and the lower part of his leg about covering the girth; the body supple, not resisting the action of the horse. The elbows should always be under the shoulders, without stiffness, and the hands should give and take, so as not at any time to have a dull, hard feeling on the horse's mouth. The leg should work in unison with the hand. It will be found that the man who rides in the position described will, in applying the leg, draw it a little back, so that the horse feels the pressure just behind the girth. The man who has good hands and seat will not, if his horse throw his head up and poke his nose out, immediately clutch the reins shorter and ram his legs or spurs into the animal's sides, but will drop his hand for a moment, and then when the horse drops his nose, as he is almost certain to do, will quietly shorten the reins a little, and close the legs so as to endeavour to keep him there.''

To remember that a man who is stiff in the saddle, and does not accompany the movements of the horse, can never have good hands, neither can the nervous rider. Both are liable to assist themselves by the reins in keeping in the saddle, and this of course makes it impossible for them to have good hands.

To be wise, if you have either of these faults incurably, and resign yourself to riding only horses to which you are accustomed and who have become used to your weaknesses.

To know, if you keep your seat well from

sheer strength, that you can make yourself hands if you choose to take the trouble; and that not to do so, and to "bully" your horses instead, is merely bad horsemanship.

To remember, if you are beginning to ride while still young, that you must sit square to the front and very upright. Learn to ride with the ball of the foot in the stirrup; never "ride home"—that is, thrusting the foot in as far as possible—never turn the foot out. Some people teach a boy to ride first without stirrups, but several great authorities consider that a boy taught in this way can never get good hands. Cavalry privates are thus trained, and they seldom have any hands. A boy has not a sufficient grip of a horse to ride without some assistance, and, naturally, if he has no other, learns to use the reins for that purpose— a fatal habit.

For a girl to learn to ride as early as a boy, and as fearlessly; she will then have every chance of becoming a really graceful horse-woman.

For her to remember that she can never become this, however constantly she may ride, unless she takes the trouble at the commencement to acquire a good seat.

For her never to forget that she must ride as square to the horse's ears as a boy, while never allowing herself to lean to one side or the other.

To take great care in the matter of fitting the stirrup. Many ladies acquire the habit of riding with a very short stirrup, and bend the left leg back so short that the sole of the boot is visible. A lady who rides in this manner almost invariably gives her horse a sore back.

To remember that the stirrup should be so adjusted that the left leg hangs down easily and almost straight, being bent just enough to allow the top of the knee to touch the under side of the pommel. The stirrup should be under the ball of the foot, not touching the ankle.

To know that, if you once acquire the habit of this seat, you sit with safety and comfort, your horse carries you with ease, and you avoid the risk of making his back sore, or contracting a lump upon your own ankle which, in a lady, is the mark of a bad rider.

Never to order your horse out in a hurry and mount him instantly if it can be avoided. Let him walk about a little, so that you know his saddle and girths are comfortable. If you find him unaccountably restive after you have started, try a look at the inside of your saddle before you begin to punish him. You may chance to find a nail working further into the horse than it has ever been into the saddle.

Not to trust your groom implicitly in all the details which affect your horse's comfort and your own safety, but to overlook them yourself.

CHAPTER II.

RIDING.

It is the correct thing

To control one's temper in dealing with a horse as well as in other relations of life. If you lose your temper, you spoil the horse's, and you yourself are, of necessity, at a disadvantage. Robert Weir observes that, while there are many comparisons to be drawn between good and bad hands and seats, the final conclusion is that the best seat and hands are in possession of the man with a good temper. Between such a one and his horse "there is, so to speak, constant communication. He has always a feeling on his horse's mouth, but never holds on

If you do not visit the stables, at all events make time to walk round your carriage when it comes to the door and see that all is in order. This is the correct thing, and your coachman will feel more respect for you if you do it, and will take more interest in his work.

If you buy carriage and horses without experience, it is the right thing to get the very best possible friendly advice you can, for these purchases are very difficult to make. You will be thought better of for asking advice than for buying foolishly.

In the same manner, it is the correct thing to visit your stables from time to time; and if you do not yourself understand the management of them, take a friend with you who does, and who can afterwards give you a hint or two. To neglect this is only to offer temptations to your grooms, and it is not fair to your horses or yourself.

In learning to drive yourself it is the correct thing to begin with one horse; to attempt more is only to invite misfortune.

To first learn to hold the reins properly, and to sit firmly and in a good position on the driving-seat. The left hand and wrist should be held straight, not stiffly, but naturally: the little finger down, the thumb and first finger uppermost. The elbows should be close to the body; to hold them square has a very bad appearance, and, besides, weakens the driver's power.

To remember that to learn to drive well requires time and patience; it is necessary to serve an apprenticeship. Sit beside a good coachman for some time, and study his methods. Then let him sit beside you while you buy your own experience and handle different kinds of horses.

To remember that a good driver is like a great artist, always learning, and ready to acquire fresh knowledge after years of work; therefore, do not imagine you can achieve all in a few weeks.

To learn all about the harness, the names and uses of its different parts. Learn this thoroughly from an old servant; then, when you have a new groom, you will be the master.

Never to mount to the box-seat without seeing for yourself that the harness is in order, the bit in its proper position, and the curb-chain neither too tight or too loose. These important details are never neglected by a workmanlike driver, however good his servants may be.

After you have driven different kinds of horses in single harness, then serve your apprenticeship with a pair; and if your ambition is to drive four-in-hand, do not attempt it until you have driven all kinds of pairs. The first necessity in driving four-in-hand is to know how to make horses of different temper do an equal amount of work.

In beginning your different apprenticeships it is the correct thing to show patience. Mistakes which arise are more likely the result of your inexperience than the horse's temper.

To drive as much as possible with one hand;

nothing is such bad form in driving as to keep the whip hand on the reins; except, perhaps, to touch the horse with the whip while both hands are on the reins. This stamps a bad driver.

To sit firmly, your feet close together, whatever may happen. To remember that this is your strongest position. The coachman who half rises when the horses get excited loses half his power.

To remember that of the two faults it is better to hold your reins three inches too short than three inches too long. If your reins are slack, you are in a very bad position if your horse stumbles or shies.

In conclusion, I will quote a few words written by the well-known tandem-driver, Lady Georgina Curzon :—

"I know nothing more delightful than to sit behind two perfectly broken horses or ponies, going well together and well in hand, passing rapidly through the air. Complete harmony exists between them and the driver, they know his hand and voice, and he understands the character of each animal. At the same time, in the hands of a skilful, experienced driver, two horses only partially trained, and in many respects somewhat raw, will also go well and with safety. Therefore, study the driving, both for your own happiness and for the pleasure you wish to give those who accompany you."

Printed by Henry Good & Son, 12, Moorgate St., London, E.C

MORE FACSIMILE REISSUES
FROM PRYOR PUBLICATIONS

THE NATURAL HISTORY OF STUCK-UP PEOPLE

'We are about to expose, as simply and truthfully as we can, the foolish conventionalities of a large proportion of the middle classes of the present day, who believe that position is attained by climbing up a staircase of moneybags'.

First published 1848   128 pages   Illustrated
ISBN: 0 946014 39 6   Paperback   Publication: August 1995
£3.99

Don't
A Manual of Mistakes and Improprieties more or less prevalent in Conduct and Speech

A best seller in the 1880s and once again in our facsimile edition (over 100,000 copies sold), *Don't* is a reflection of a society long since past, and makes for fascinating and amusing reading now.
£3.50

12 pages   ISBN: 0 946014 02 7   Paperback

ENGLISH AS SHE IS SPOKE
OR A JEST IN SOBER EARNEST

This book derives from Pedro Carolino's 'Guide to the Conversation in Portuguese and English' published in 1869. It shows that Carolino's knowledge of English was little more than that furnished by a French-English dictionary and was a greater contribution to humour than linguistics!

First published 1885   80 pages   ISBN: 0 946014 09 4   Paperback
£3.50

MANNERS FOR MEN

Mrs Humphry, who is also the author of *Manners for Women*, wrote 'Like ever
other woman I have my ideal of manhood. The difficulty is to describe it. Firs
of all, he must be a gentleman, but that means so much that it, in its turr
requires explanation . . .'

First published 1897   176 pages
ISBN: 0 946014 23 X   Paperback

£4.50

MANNERS FOR WOMEN

Can anything be nicer than a really nice girl? 'may seem quaint but it is
useful reminder that tittering is an unpleasant habit and curtseying shoul
be avoided unless you know what you are doing.' *The Times.*

First published 1897   164 pages
ISBN: 0 946014 17 5   Paperback

£3.9ᵉ

What Shall I Say?

A guide to letter writing for ladies first published in 1898.
132 pages   ISBN: 0 946014 25 6   Paperback

£3.50

MASTER YOUR MOODS

Subtitled 'Philosophy for Daily Life' quotations from writers includir
Bacon, Socrates and Dr Johnson will help when you are feeling ange
worry, envy or just about any other emotion.

First published 1885   64 pages   ISBN: 0 946014 34 5   Paperback

£3.50

A SHORT HISTORY OF THE WOLF IN BRITAIN

Taken from James Harting's 'British Animals Extinct Within Moder
Times', first published in 1880, here are early accounts of the wolf in th
British Isles until its demise around 1760.

96 pages   Illustrated   ISBN: 0 946014 27 2   Paperback

£5.9

OUR NATIVE ENGLAND
BEING THE HISTORY OF ENGLAND MADE EASY

For each ruler from Egbert to Victoria, and also including tribes from the Britons to Jutes and Angles, this little book instructs and informs with woodcuts and brief descriptions in rhyme.

First published 1838   64 pages   47 woodcuts
ISBN: 0 946014 19 1   Paperback

£2.99

HAND SHADOWS

A delightful resurrection of an amusing and educational pastime now sadly neglected — the perfect antidote to today's rush and bustle.

First published 1860   48 pages   Illustrated
ISBN: 0 946014 24 8   Paperback

£3.99

EVERYBODY'S BOOK OF EPITAPHS

BEING FOR THE MOST PART WHAT THE LIVING THINK OF THE DEAD

Here lies my wife, a sad slattern and shrew
If I said I regretted her, I should lie too!

A look at epitaphs for the famous to the poor — some amusing, some sad, some historic, some enlightening, all fascinating.

Originally published 1885.
3.5cm x 10.5cm   128 pages
Paperback   ISBN: 0 946014 38 8

£4.50

Available from bookshops or post free from
PRYOR PUBLICATIONS
75 Dargate Road, Yorkletts, Whitstable, Kent CT5 3AE, England.
Tel. & Fax: (01227) 274655
A full list of our publications sent free on request